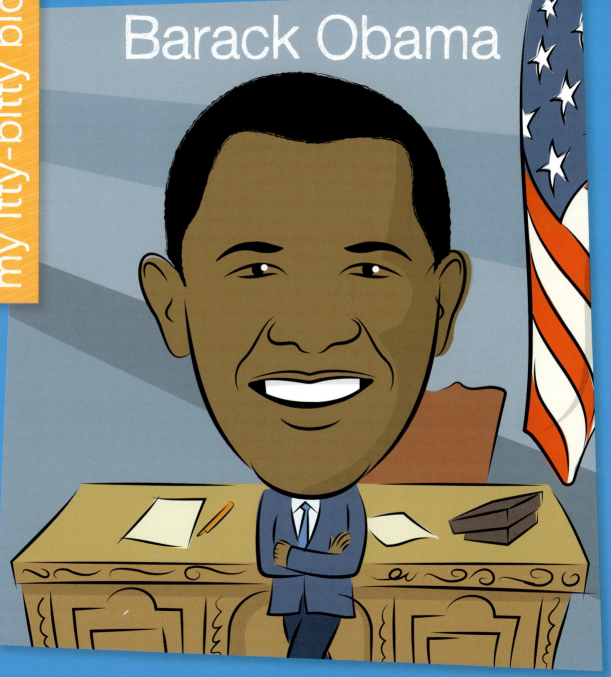

my itty-bitty bio

Barack Obama

Published in the United States of America by Cherry Lake Publishing Group
Ann Arbor, Michigan
www.cherrylakepublishing.com

Reading Adviser: Beth Walker Gambro, MS, Ed., Reading Consultant, Yorkville, IL
Book Designer: Jennifer Wahi
Illustrator: Jeff Bane

Photo Credits: © U.S. Embassy, Jakarta/flickr, 5; ©fizkes/Shutterstock, 7; © Jay Yuan/Shutterstock, 9; ©U.S. Embassy, Jakarta/flickr, 11; ©Photo by David Katz/Office of Senator Barack Obama/Wikimedia, 13, 22; ©Obama Library/V110612DL-1118, 15; ©Obama Library/P112310PS-1414, 17; ©Obama Library/P021413PS-0294, 19; ©Obama Library/P040515PS-0034, 21, 23; Cover, 1, 8, 12, 14, Jeff Bane; Various frames throughout, Shutterstock

Copyright ©2022 by Cherry Lake Publishing Group
All rights reserved. No part of this book may be reproduced or utilized in any form or by any means without written permission from the publisher.

Cherry Lake Press is an imprint of Cherry Lake Publishing Group.

Library of Congress Cataloging-in-Publication Data

Names: Sarantou, Katlin, author. | Bane, Jeff, 1957- illustrator.
Title: Barack Obama / Katlin Sarantou ; illustrated by Jeff Bane.
Description: Ann Arbor, Michigan : Cherry Lake Publishing, [2021] | Series: My itty-bitty bio | Includes index.
Identifiers: LCCN 2021007973 (print) | LCCN 2021007974 (ebook) | ISBN 9781534186903 (hardcover) | ISBN 9781534188303 (paperback) | ISBN 9781534189706 (pdf) | ISBN 9781534191105 (ebook)
Subjects: LCSH: Obama, Barack--Juvenile literature. | Presidents--United States--Biography--Juvenile literature. | African American politicians--Biography--Juvenile literature. | Politicians--United States--Biography--Juvenile literature.
Classification: LCC E908 .S27 2021 (print) | LCC E908 (ebook) | DDC 973.932092 [B]--dc23
LC record available at https://lccn.loc.gov/2021007973
LC ebook record available at https://lccn.loc.gov/2021007974

Printed in the United States of America
Corporate Graphics

table of contents

My Story 4

Timeline 22

Glossary 24

Index 24

About the author: Katlin Sarantou grew up in the cornfields of Ohio. She enjoys reading and dreaming of faraway places.

About the illustrator: Jeff Bane and his two business partners own a studio along the American River in Folsom, California, home of the 1849 Gold Rush. When Jeff's not sketching or illustrating for clients, he's either swimming or kayaking in the river to relax.

my story

I was born in Hawaii. The year was 1961. My mom was White. My dad was Black.

I noticed my **race** as a child. Other kids didn't look like me.

But I learned we're all different. And that's okay.

I went to Harvard University.
I was the first Black president of the Harvard Law Review.

I became a **civil rights attorney**.

I met Michelle in 1989. We were married in 1992.

We have two daughters. I'm proud to be their dad.

What are you proud of?

I became a state **senator** in 1997.

Then I became a U.S. senator in 2005.

I was elected president of the United States in 2008.

I was the first African American president.

I passed many bills. I made **health care affordable**.

Same-sex marriage became legal. **LGBTQ+** people in the military were able to serve openly.

I still wanted to help people after I was president.

I started the Obama Foundation.

How can you help people?

I've won the Nobel Peace Prize.
I've written books. I've traveled the world.

I'm happiest when I'm with my family.

What would you like to ask me?

timeline

2005

1960

↑
Born
1961

2009

2060

glossary

affordable (uh-FOR-duh-buhl) low-cost

attorney (uh-TUR-nee) a lawyer, someone who practices the law

civil rights (SIV-il RITES) the rights of a person guaranteed by the Constitution

health care (HELTH KAIR) access to doctors and medicine

LGBTQ+ (ELL GEE BEE TEE KYU PLUS) lesbian, gay, bisexual, transgender, queer, and more

race (RAYSS) physical traits, like skin color

senator (SEH-nuh-tuhr) an elected official who helps pass laws

index

Black, 4, 8, 14

civil rights attorney, 8

Harvard University, 8
Hawaii, 4

legal, 16
LGBTQ+, 16

married, 10
military, 16

Obama Foundation, 18

president, 8, 14, 18

senator, 12